POPULAR SONGS
HAL LEONARD STUDENT PIANO LIBRARY

Hal Leonard
7777 West Bluemound Road
Milwaukee, WI 53213
Email: info@halleonard.com

T0056015

Smash Hits

Arranged by Mona Rejino

ISBN 978-1-5400-3743-5

HAL•LEONARD®

Visit Hal Leonard Online at
www.halleonard.com

Contact us:
Hal Leonard
7777 West Bluemound Road
Milwaukee, WI 53213
Email: info@halleonard.com

In Europe, contact:
Hal Leonard Europe Limited
42 Wigmore Street
Marylebone, London, W1U 2RN
Email: info@halleonardeurope.com

In Australia, contact:
Hal Leonard Australia Pty. Ltd.
4 Lentara Court
Cheltenham, Victoria, 3192 Australia
Email: info@halleonard.com.au

From the Arranger

We all enjoy playing current popular hits on the piano, making the music we listen to our own. *Smash Hits* includes many styles and genres, giving you the opportunity to show your musical diversity. "The Middle," "There's Nothing Holdin' Me Back," and "No Tears Left to Cry" all share a driving intensity and strong beat. "Perfect" feels like a laidback ballad. "Meant to Be" gives you a taste of country, while "Havana" adds a memorable Latin flair to the mix. "Evermore" and "A Million Dreams" whisk you away with their beautiful, sweeping melodies. Try to capture the unique mood of each piece, and share this music with others.

Mona Rejino

An accomplished pianist, composer, arranger, and teacher, **Mona Rejino** maintains an independent piano studio in Carrollton, Texas. She also teaches privately at the Hockaday School and is a frequent adjudicator in the Dallas area. A member of *Who's Who of American Women*, Mona received her music degrees from West Texas State University and the University of North Texas. She and her husband, Richard, often present programs on a variety of topics for music teacher associations throughout Texas as well as nationally.

CONTENTS

Evermore

from BEAUTY AND THE BEAST

Music by Alan Menken
Lyrics by Tim Rice
Arranged by Mona Rejino

Moderately slow, with freedom (♩ = c. 92)

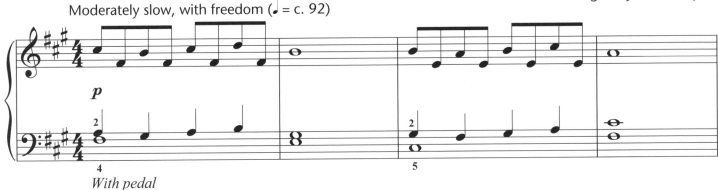

p

With pedal

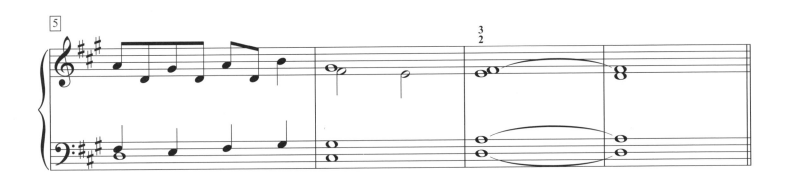

Sturdy Ballad

mp I was the one ___ who had it all;
I'll nev - er shake ___ a - way the pain.

I was the mas - ter of my
I close my eyes, ___ but she's still

fate.
there.

I nev - er need - ed an - y - bod - y in my life;
I let her steal in - to my mel - an - chol - y heart;

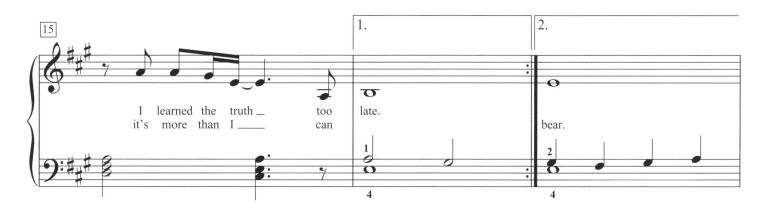

I learned the truth __ too late.
it's more than I ____ can bear.

Now I know she'll nev - er leave me, e - ven as she runs a -

way. She will still tor - ment __ me, calm me, hurt __ me, move me, come what

may. Wast - ing in __ my lone - ly tow - er, _____

waiting by ___ an o - pen door, I'll fool my - self she'll walk right

in, and be with me for ev - er - more.

I rage a - gainst ___ the trials of love. I curse the fad - ing of the

light. Though she's al - read - y flown so far be - yond my reach,

she's nev - er out of sight. *rit.* **f** Now I know she'll nev - er *a tempo*

leave me, e - ven as she fades from view. She will

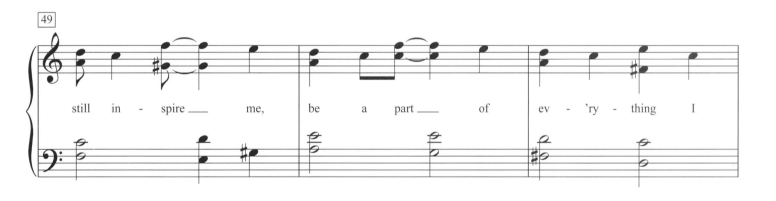

still in - spire ___ me, be a part ___ of ev - 'ry - thing I

do. Wast - ing in my lone - ly tow - er,

waiting by an o - pen door,

dim.

mp

I'll fool my-self she'll walk right in,

and as the long, long nights be - gin,

cresc. poco a poco

I'll think of all that might have

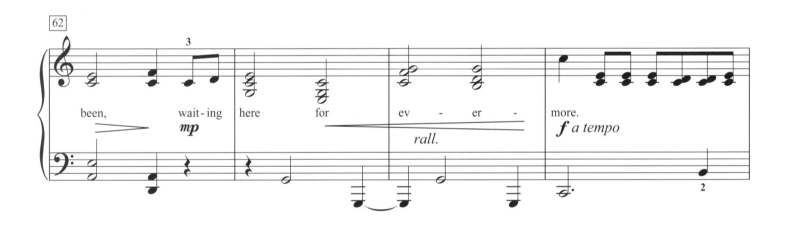

been, waiting here for ev - er - more.

mp

rall.

f a tempo

rall.

The Middle

Words and Music by Sarah Aarons,
Marcus Lomax, Jordan Johnson,
Anton Zaslavski, Kyle Trewartha,
Michael Trewartha and Stefan Johnson
Arranged by Mona Rejino

Moderately (♩ = c. 104)

Take a seat right o-ver there, sat on the stairs. Stay or leave, the

cab-'nets are bare and I'm un-a-ware of just how we got in-to this mess, got so ag-gres-sive.

I know we meant all good in-ten-tions, so pull me clos-er. Why don't you pull me

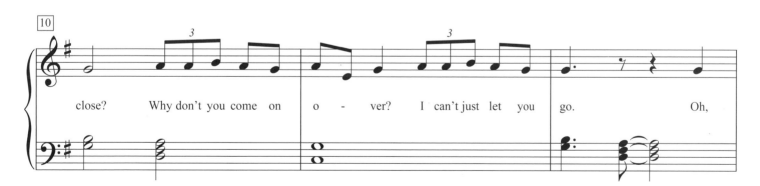

close? Why don't you come on o-ver? I can't just let you go. Oh,

Havana

Words and Music by Camila Cabello,
Louis Bell, Pharrell Williams,
Adam Feeney, Ali Tamposi, Brian Lee,
Andrew Wotman, Brittany Hazzard,
Jeffery Lamar Williams and Kaan Gunesberk
Arranged by Mona Rejino

With a Latin groove (♩ = c. 104)

Ha - van - a, ooh na na.   Half of my heart is in Ha-

van - a, ooh na na.   He took me back to East At - lan - ta, na na na.

To Coda

Ah, but my heart is in Ha - van - a, {there's some-thing 'bout his / my heart is in Ha- } man - ners. Ha - van - a, ooh. He

van - a, Ha-van - a, ooh na | Ooh na na na, ___ ooh na na | na. Take me back, back, back. ___

mp

Ooh na na na, ___ ooh na na | na. Take me back, back, back. ___ | na. Take me back, back, back.

1. **2.**

(Trumpet solo)

Ooh. _____ Ooh. _____ Ha-

16

van - a, ooh na na. Half of my heart is in Ha - van - a, ooh na na.

He took me back to East At - lan - ta, na na na. Ah, but my heart is in Ha -

van - a, my heart is in Ha - van - a, Ha-van-a, ooh na na. Ooh na na na.

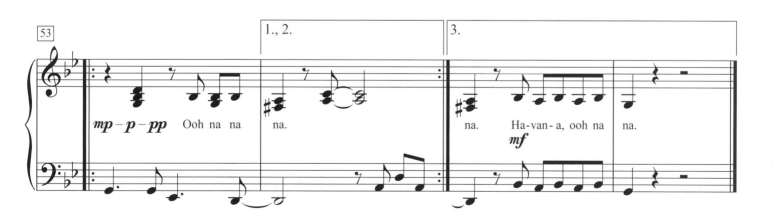

mp – p – pp Ooh na na na. na. Ha-van - a, ooh na na. *mf*

Meant to Be

Words and Music by Bleta Rexha,
Josh Miller, Tyler Hubbard
and David Garcia
Arranged by Mona Rejino

Moderately, in 2 (♩ = c. 76)

With pedal

lay on back and re - lax. ___ Kick your pret - ty feet ___ up on my dash. ___ No

need to go no - where fast. ___ Let's en - joy ___ right here where we're at. Who

knows where this road is sup - posed to lead? ___ We got noth - in' but time. ___ ___ As

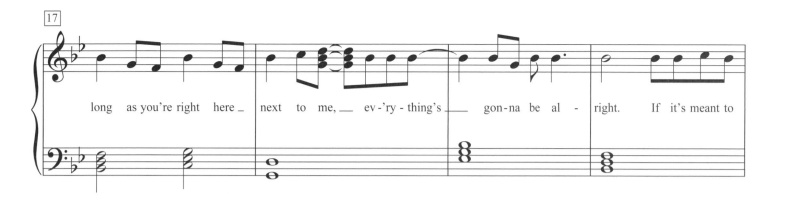

long as you're right here _ next to me, _ ev-'ry-thing's _ gon-na be al - right. If it's meant to

be, it-'ll be, _ it-'ll be. _ Ba - by, just let it be. _ If it's meant to

be, it-'ll be, _ it-'ll be. _ Ba - by, just let it be. _ So, won't you

ride with me, ride with me? See where this thing goes. If it's meant to

Whoa, hold up, ___ girl. Don't you know you're beau-ti - ful? And it's eas - y to see. ___ If it's meant to

be, it - 'll be, ___ it - 'll be. Ba - by, just let it be. ___ If it's meant to

be, it - 'll be, ___ it - 'll be. Ba - by, just let it be. ___ So won't you

ride with me, ride with me? See where this thing goes. If it's meant to

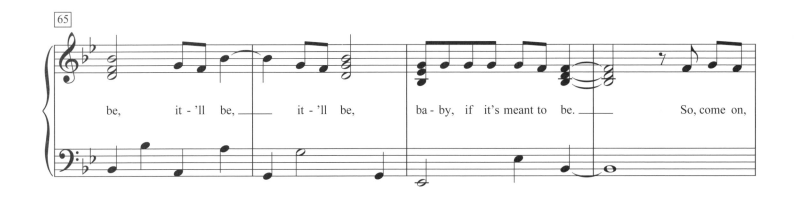

be, it -'ll be, ___ it -'ll be. Ba - by, just let it be. ___ If it's meant to

be, it -'ll be, ___ it -'ll be. Ba - by, just let it be. ___ So, won't you

f

ride with me, ride with me? See where this thing goes. If it's meant to

be, it -'ll be, ___ it -'ll be, ba - by, if it's meant to be. ___

No Tears Left to Cry

Words and Music by Ariana Grande,
Savan Kotecha, Max Martin and Ilya
Arranged by Mona Rejino

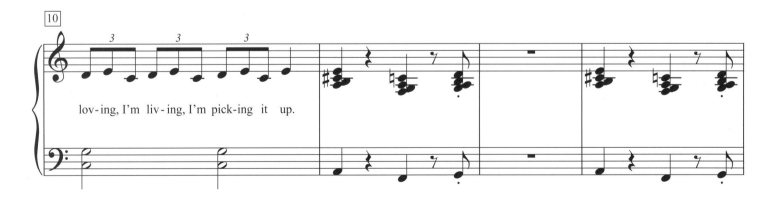

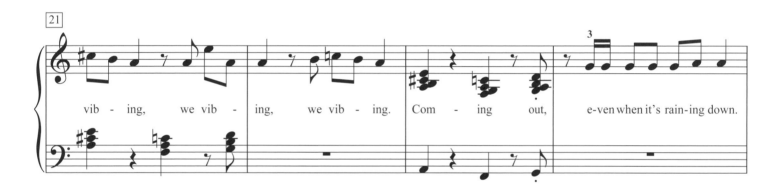

Perfect

Words and Music by
Ed Sheeran
Arranged by Mona Rejino

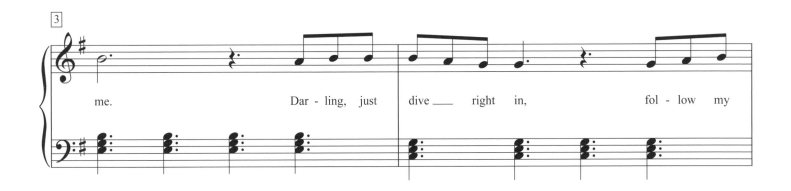

me. _____ 'Cause we were just kids when we
so _____ in _____ love, fight - ing a -

what _____ it was. I will not give you _____ up this
gainst _____ all odds. I know we'll be all _____ right this

time. _____ Dar - ling, just kiss me slow, your heart is
time. _____ Dar - ling, just hold my hand. Be my girl, I'll

all I own. And in your eyes, you're _____ hold - ing mine. ___
be your man. I've seen the fu - ture _____ in your eyes. ___

Ba - by, _____ I'm danc - ing in the dark with you be - tween my

arms. Bare - foot on the grass, lis - ten - ing to our

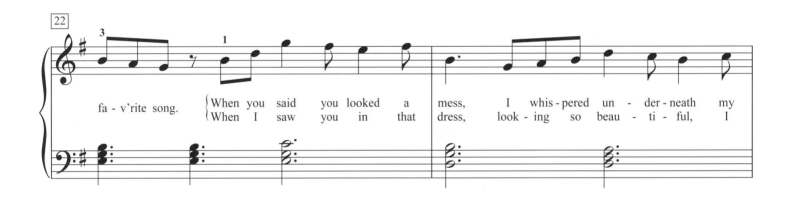

fa - v'rite song. When you said you looked a mess, I whis - pered un - der - neath my
When I saw you in that dress, look - ing so beau - ti - ful, I

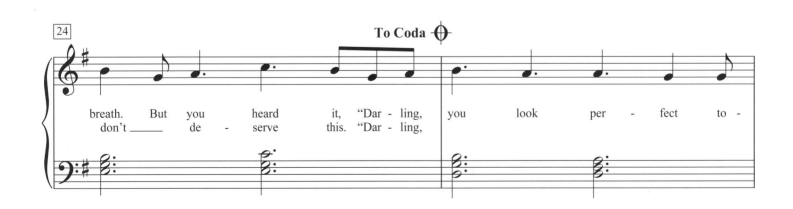

To Coda ⊕

breath. But you heard it, "Dar - ling, you look per - fect to -
don't _____ de - serve this. "Dar - ling,

night."

Well, I found a wom - an, _____ strong - er than

an - y - one I know. She shares my dreams, I hope _____ that some - day, I'll share her

home. _____ I found a love _____ to car - ry more than just my se - crets, to car - ry

D.S. al Coda

love, to car - ry chil - dren _____ of our own. _____ We are still kids, but we're

CODA

you look per - fect to - night."

Ba - by, _____ I'm _____ danc - ing in the

dark _____ with you be - tween my arms. Bare - foot on the

grass, lis - ten - ing to our fa - v'rite song. I have faith in what __ I

see, now I know I have met an an - gel in per - son and

she looks per - fect. I don't de - serve this, you look per - fect to-

night.

rit.

There's Nothing Holdin' Me Back

Words and Music by Shawn Mendes,
Geoffrey Warburton, Teddy Geiger
and Scott Harris
Arranged by Mona Rejino

Acoustic Pop (♩ = c. 120)

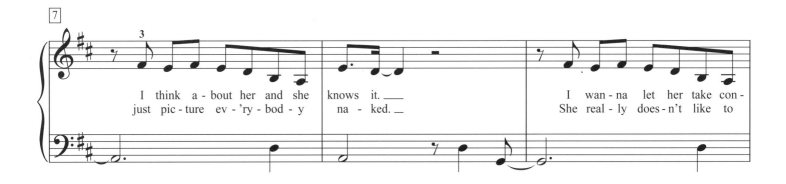

A Million Dreams

from THE GREATEST SHOWMAN

Words and Music by Benj Pasek
and Justin Paul
Arranged by Mona Rejino

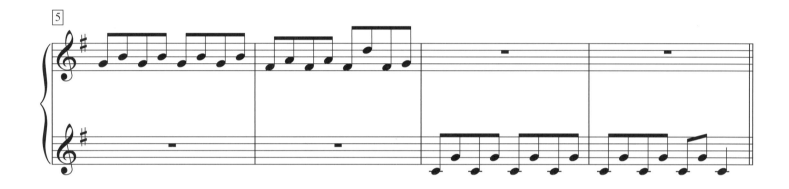

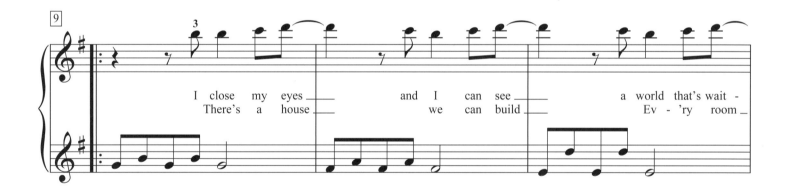

I close my eyes and I can see a world that's wait -
There's a house we can build Ev - 'ry room

- ing up for me that I call my own
in - side is filled with things from far a - way

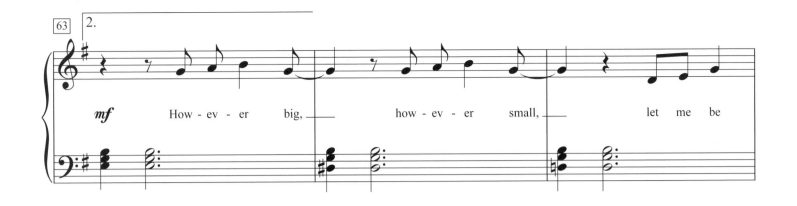

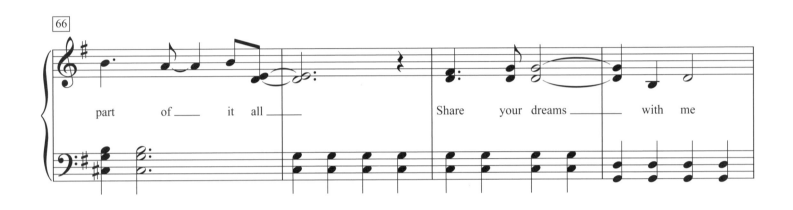

world I close my eyes to see, _____ I close my eyes to see _

_____ 'Cause ev - 'ry night _ I lie _____ in bed _____ the

bright - est col - ors fill my head A mil - lion dreams _ are keep -

- in' me _ a - wake _____ A mil - ion dreams, _ a mil - lion dreams _ I

POPULAR SONGS
HAL LEONARD
STUDENT PIANO LIBRARY

The **Hal Leonard Student Piano Library** has great songs, and you will find all your favorites here: Disney classics, Broadway and movie favorites, and today's top hits. These graded collections are skillfully and imaginatively arranged for students and pianists at every level, from elementary solos with teacher accompaniments to sophisticated piano solos for the advancing pianist.

Adele
arr. Mona Rejino
00159590 Correlates with HLSPL Level 5...........$12.99

The Beatles
arr. Eugénie Rocherolle
00296649 Correlates with HLSPL Level 5...........$10.99

Irving Berlin Piano Duos
arr. Don Heitler and Jim Lyke
00296838 Correlates with HLSPL Level 5...........$14.99

Broadway Hits
arr. Carol Klose
00296650 Correlates with HLSPL Levels 4/5........$8.99

Chart Hits
arr. Mona Rejino
00296710 Correlates with HLSPL Level 5.............$8.99

Christmas Cheer
arr. Phillip Keveren
00296616 Correlates with HLSPL Level 4.............$6.95

Classic Christmas Favorites
arr. Jennifer & Mike Watts
00129582 Correlates with HLSPL Level 5.............$9.99

Christmas Time Is Here
arr. Eugénie Rocherolle
00296614 Correlates with HLSPL Level 5.............$8.99

Classic Joplin Rags
arr. Fred Kern
00296743 Correlates with HLSPL Level 5.............$9.99

**Classical Pop –
Lady Gaga Fugue & Other Pop Hits**
arr. Giovanni Dettori
00296921 Correlates with HLSPL Level 5...........$12.99

Contemporary Movie Hits
arr. by Carol Klose, Jennifer Linn and Wendy Stevens
00296780 Correlates with HLSPL Level 5.............$8.99

Contemporary Pop Hits
arr. Wendy Stevens
00296836 Correlates with HLSPL Level 3.............$8.99

Country Favorites
arr. Mona Rejino
00296861 Correlates with HLSPL Level 5.............$9.99

Current Hits
arr. Mona Rejino
00296768 Correlates with HLSPL Level 5.............$8.99

Disney Favorites
arr. Phillip Keveren
00296647 Correlates with HLSPL Levels 3/4........$9.99

Disney Film Favorites
arr. Mona Rejino
00296809 Correlates with HLSPL Level 5...........$10.99

Easy Christmas Duets
arr. Mona Rejino and Phillip Keveren
00237139 Correlates with HLSPL Level 3/4 ....$9.99

Four Hands on Broadway
arr. Fred Kern
00146177 Correlates with HLSPL Level 5...........$12.99

Jazz Hits for Piano Duet
arr. Jeremy Siskind
00143248 Correlates with HLSPL Level 5 ....$10.99

Elton John
arr. Carol Klose
00296721 Correlates with HLSPL Level 5.............$8.99

Joplin Ragtime Duets
arr. Fred Kern
00296771 Correlates with HLSPL Level 5.............$8.99

Jerome Kern Classics
arr. Eugénie Rocherolle
00296577 Correlates with HLSPL Level 5...........$12.99

Pop Hits for Piano Duet
arr. Jeremy Siskind
00224734 Correlates with HLSPL Level 5...........$10.99

Sing to the King
arr. Phillip Keveren
00296808 Correlates with HLSPL Level 5.............$8.99

Spooky Halloween Tunes
arr. Fred Kern
00121550 Correlates with HLSPL Levels 3/4........$9.99

Today's Hits
arr. Mona Rejino
00296646 Correlates with HLSPL Level 5.............$7.99

Top Hits
arr. Jennifer and Mike Watts
00296894 Correlates with HLSPL Level 5...........$10.99

Top Piano Ballads
arr. Jennifer Watts
00197926 Correlates with HLSPL Level 5...........$10.99

You Raise Me Up
arr. Deborah Brady
00296576 Correlates with HLSPL Levels 2/3........$7.95

HAL•LEONARD®
7777 W. BLUEMOUND RD. P.O. BOX 13819 MILWAUKEE, WI 53213

Visit our website at www.halleonard.com

Prices, contents and availability subject to change without notice. Prices may vary outside the U.S.

COMPOSER SHOWCASE
HAL LEONARD STUDENT PIANO LIBRARY

This series showcases great original piano music from our **Hal Leonard Student Piano Library** family of composers. Carefully graded for easy selection.

BILL BOYD

JAZZ BITS (AND PIECES)
Early Intermediate Level
00290312 11 Solos.............................$7.99
JAZZ DELIGHTS
Intermediate Level
00240435 11 Solos.............................$7.99
JAZZ FEST
Intermediate Level
00240436 10 Solos.............................$8.99
JAZZ PRELIMS
Early Elementary Level
00290032 12 Solos.............................$7.99
JAZZ SKETCHES
Intermediate Level
00220001 8 Solos.............................$8.99
JAZZ STARTERS
Elementary Level
00290425 10 Solos.............................$7.99
JAZZ STARTERS II
Late Elementary Level
00290434 11 Solos.............................$7.99
JAZZ STARTERS III
Late Elementary Level
00290465 12 Solos.............................$8.99
THINK JAZZ!
Early Intermediate Level
00290417 Method Book.............................$12.99

TONY CARAMIA

JAZZ MOODS
Intermediate Level
00296728 8 Solos.............................$6.95
SUITE DREAMS
Intermediate Level
00296775 4 Solos.............................$6.99

SONDRA CLARK

THREE ODD METERS
Intermediate Level
00296472 3 Duets.............................$6.95

MATTHEW EDWARDS

CONCERTO FOR YOUNG PIANISTS
FOR 2 PIANOS, FOUR HANDS
Intermediate Level Book/CD
00296356 3 Movements.............................$19.99
CONCERTO NO. 2 IN G MAJOR
FOR 2 PIANOS, 4 HANDS
Intermediate Level Book/CD
00296670 3 Movements.............................$17.99

PHILLIP KEVEREN

MOUSE ON A MIRROR
Late Elementary Level
00296361 5 Solos.............................$7.99
MUSICAL MOODS
Elementary/Late Elementary Level
00296714 7 Solos.............................$5.95
SHIFTY-EYED BLUES
Late Elementary Level
00296374 5 Solos.............................$7.99

CAROL KLOSE

THE BEST OF CAROL KLOSE
Early Intermediate to Late Intermediate Level
00146151 15 Solos.............................$12.99
CORAL REEF SUITE
Late Elementary Level
00296354 7 Solos.............................$6.99
DESERT SUITE
Intermediate Level
00296667 6 Solos.............................$7.99
FANCIFUL WALTZES
Early Intermediate Level
00296473 5 Solos.............................$7.95
GARDEN TREASURES
Late Intermediate Level
00296787 5 Solos.............................$7.99
ROMANTIC EXPRESSIONS
Intermediate/Late Intermediate Level
00296923 5 Solos.............................$8.99
WATERCOLOR MINIATURES
Early Intermediate Level
00296848 7 Solos.............................$7.99

JENNIFER LINN

AMERICAN IMPRESSIONS
Intermediate Level
00296471 6 Solos.............................$8.99
ANIMALS HAVE FEELINGS TOO
Early Elementary/Elementary Level
00147789 8 Solos.............................$7.99
CHRISTMAS IMPRESSIONS
Intermediate Level
00296706 8 Solos.............................$8.99
JUST PINK
Elementary Level
00296722 9 Solos.............................$8.99
LES PETITES IMAGES
Late Elementary Level
00296664 7 Solos.............................$8.99
LES PETITES IMPRESSIONS
Intermediate Level
00296355 6 Solos.............................$7.99
REFLECTIONS
Late Intermediate Level
00296843 5 Solos.............................$7.99
TALES OF MYSTERY
Intermediate Level
00296769 6 Solos.............................$8.99

LYNDA LYBECK-ROBINSON

ALASKA SKETCHES
Early Intermediate Level
00119637 8 Solos.............................$7.99
AN AWESOME ADVENTURE
Late Elementary Level
00137563.............................$7.99
FOR THE BIRDS
Early Intermediate/Intermediate Level
00237078.............................$8.99
WHISPERING WOODS
Late Elementary Level
00275905 9 Solos.............................$8.99

MONA REJINO

CIRCUS SUITE
Late Elementary Level
00296665 5 Solos.............................$6.99
COLOR WHEEL
Early Intermediate Level
00201951 6 Solos.............................$8.99
JUST FOR KIDS
Elementary Level
00296840 8 Solos.............................$7.99
MERRY CHRISTMAS MEDLEYS
Intermediate Level
00296799 5 Solos.............................$8.99
MINIATURES IN STYLE
Intermediate Level
00148088 6 Solos.............................$8.99
PORTRAITS IN STYLE
Early Intermediate Level
00296507 6 Solos.............................$8.99

EUGÉNIE ROCHEROLLE

CELEBRATION SUITE
Intermediate Level
00152724 3 Duets (1 Piano, 4 Hands)...............$8.99
**ENCANTOS ESPAÑOLES
(SPANISH DELIGHTS)**
Intermediate Level
00125451 6 Solos.............................$8.99
JAMBALAYA
Intermediate Level
00296654 Ensemble (2 Pianos, 8 Hands)........$10.99
JAMBALAYA
Intermediate Level
00296725 Piano Duo (2 Pianos).......................$7.95
LITTLE BLUES CONCERTO
FOR 2 PIANOS, 4 HANDS
Early Intermediate Level
00142801 Piano Duo (2 Pianos, 4 Hands)........$12.99
TOUR FOR TWO
Late Elementary Level
00296832 6 Duets.............................$7.99
TREASURES
Late Elementary/Early Intermediate Level
00296924 7 Solos.............................$8.99

JEREMY SISKIND

BIG APPLE JAZZ
Intermediate Level
00278209 8 Solos.............................$8.99
MYTHS AND MONSTERS
Late Elementary/Early Intermediate Level
00148148 9 Solos.............................$7.99

CHRISTOS TSITSAROS

DANCES FROM AROUND THE WORLD
Early Intermediate Level
00296688 7 Solos.............................$6.95
LYRIC BALLADS
Intermediate/Late Intermediate Level
00102404 6 Solos.............................$8.99
POETIC MOMENTS
Intermediate Level
00296403 8 Solos.............................$8.99
SEA DIARY
Early Intermediate Level
00253486 9 Solos.............................$8.99
SONATINA HUMORESQUE
Late Intermediate Level
00296772 3 Movements.............................$6.99
SONGS WITHOUT WORDS
Intermediate Level
00296506 9 Solos.............................$9.99
THREE PRELUDES
Early Advanced Level
00130747.............................$8.99
THROUGHOUT THE YEAR
Late Elementary Level
00296723 12 Duets.............................$6.95

ADDITIONAL COLLECTIONS

AMERICAN PORTRAITS
by Wendy Stevens
Intermediate Level
00296817 6 Solos.............................$7.99
AT THE LAKE
by Elvina Pearce
Elementary/Late Elementary Level
00131642 10 Solos and Duets.............................$7.99
COUNTY RAGTIME FESTIVAL
by Fred Kern
Intermediate Level
00296882 7 Rags.............................$7.99
LITTLE JAZZERS
by Jennifer Watts
Elementary/Late Elementary Level
00154573 Solos.............................8.99
PLAY THE BLUES!
by Luann Carman (Method Book)
Early Intermediate Level
00296357 10 Solos.............................$9.99

Prices, contents, and availability subject
to change without notice.

HAL•LEONARD®

www.halleonard.com

0518